Ela Area
275 Mohawk ~~~~
(847) 438-3433
www.eapl.org

31241010299447

AUG − − 2020

ORIENTAL CATS

by Mary Ellen Klukow

AMICUS | AMICUS INK

Amicus High Interest and Amicus Ink are published by Amicus
P.O. Box 1329, Mankato, MN 56002
www.amicuspublishing.us

Copyright © 2020 Amicus. International copyright reserved in all countries. No part of this book may be reproduced in any form without written permission from the publisher.

Library of Congress Cataloging-in-Publication Data
Names: Klukow, Mary Ellen, author.
Title: Oriental cats / by Mary Ellen Klukow.
Description: Mankato, Minnesota : Amicus/Amicus Ink, [2020] | Series:
  Favorite cat breeds | Audience: K to Grade 3. | Includes index.
Identifiers: LCCN 2018049611 (print) | LCCN 2018050314 (ebook) | ISBN
  9781681518589 (pdf) | ISBN 9781681518183 (library binding) | ISBN
  9781681525464 (paperback)
Subjects: LCSH: Oriental cat—Juvenile literature. | Cat breeds—Juvenile
  literature.
Classification: LCC SF449.O73 (ebook) | LCC SF449.O73 K58 2020 (print) |
  DDC 636.8—dc23
LC record available at https://lccn.loc.gov/2018049611

Photo Credits: iStock/GlobalP cover; Dreamstime/Jagodka 2;
Shutterstock/TalyaPhoto 5; AgeFotostock/Medici 6–7; iStock/GlobalP 8;
Shutterstock/Reva Vera 10–11; iStock/GlobalP 12–13; Polly E Perkins/@
polyphemus.polly/Flickr/polyphemus_polly 14; iStock/Marina Zharinova
16–17; Shutterstock/TalyaPhoto 18–19; Shutterstock/Julia Pivovarova 21;
iStock/nelik 22–23

Editor: Alissa Thielges
Designer: Ciara Beitlich
Photo Researchers: Holly Young and Shane Freed

Printed in the United States of America

HC 10 9 8 7 6 5 4 3 2 1
PB 10 9 8 7 6 5 4 3 2 1

TABLE OF CONTENTS

A FUN CAT

Two big eyes are looking right at you. It is an Oriental Shorthair cat. He nudges you with his head. He wants to play! Orientals are a fun-loving cat breed.

5

HISTORY

Oriental cats come from England.
The breed was created in the
1900s. Breeders combined
Siamese cats with other breeds.
The result was the Oriental.

Siamese

⑧

THIN ALL OVER

Orientals are long and **slender**. They have skinny tails and long legs. Their ears and eyes are big, but their faces are thin. Orientals are known for looking graceful.

Fun Fact
There is an Oriental Longhair breed, too. Those cats have a longer coat.

COLORFUL COATS

Orientals look like Siamese cats. But Siamese cats are only two colors. Orientals can be many colors. They can be one solid color or have a pattern with different colors.

Fun Fact
Orientals can have over 300 kinds of coat patterns.

PLAYFUL KITTIES

Orientals aren't just fun cats. They are smart, too. They like to play games. Boxes and strings are some of their favorite toys. Some Orientals even play fetch!

13

FLEXIBLE

Look at that Oriental all curled up and sleeping. Oriental cats are **flexible**. They can bend their bodies easily. They like to squeeze into small spaces.

CHATTY CATS

Oriental cats are **chatty**. They make a lot of noises. They like to "talk." Orientals have **raspy** voices. Their meows have a unique sound.

Like a Wild Cat?
Cheetahs are the only big cats that can meow. They meow to talk to each other.

CURIOUS KITTENS

An Oriental kitten is **active**. As soon as her eyes open, she explores her world. She crawls around. She scratches with her claws. She plays with other kittens.

Like a Wild Cat?
Lynx kittens explore, too. They learn from their mother.

LOVING AND FRIENDLY

Oriental cats love to be the center of attention. They need lots of love. They give lots of love back, too. Orientals like being part of a big family. They make great pets!

HOW DO YOU KNOW IT'S AN ORIENTAL?

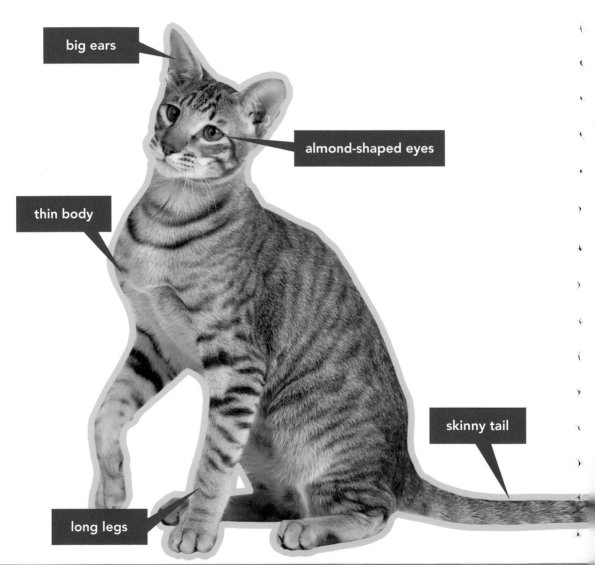

big ears

almond-shaped eyes

thin body

skinny tail

long legs

WORDS TO KNOW

active – energetic and busy, moving around often

chatty – fond of talking or communicating

flexible – able to bend easily

raspy – rough or hoarse, usually in talking about a voice

slender – gracefully thin or slim

LEARN MORE

Books

Amstutz, Lisa. *Cats*. North Mankato, Minn.: Capstone Press, 2018.

Brown, Domini. *Orientals*. Minneapolis: Bellwether Media, 2016.

Finne, Stephanie. *Oriental Shorthair Cats*. Minneapolis: Abdo Publishing, 2015.

Websites

CFA: About the Oriental
http://cfa.org/Breeds/BreedsKthruR/Oriental.aspx

Science Kids: Cats
http://www.sciencekids.co.nz/sciencefacts/animals/cat.html

INDEX

Every effort has been made to ensure that these websites are appropriate for children. However, because of the nature of the Internet, it is impossible to guarantee that these sites will remain active indefinitely or that their contents will not be altered.